RICHMOND
photographs

TONY ARNOLD

TOPAZ BOOKS

RICHMOND
photographs

A PHOTOGRAPHIC PORTRAIT OF RICHMOND UPON THAMES, SURREY.

TONY ARNOLD

For Isabelle and Max
with all my love

Acknowledgements:

To my wife, Isabelle for her support at all times
To my mother Pamela and late father Patrick

Also for all your help Robin, at C+H

First Published in Great Britain by Topaz Books
www.topazbooks.co.uk

13- digit ISBN: 978 0 9556963 0 5

Tony Arnold is hereby identified as the author of this work in accordance with Section 77 of The
Copyright , Designs an
Patents Act 1988

Printed and bound in Singapore by Star Standard Industries Limited
photographs all copyright tony arnold 2007 www.arnold-photo.co.uk +
design and layout topaz books 2007

Having grown up and lived most of his life in and around Richmond Tony Arnold has created a photographic portait of this beautiful town on the Thames. The photographs in this book were taken between 1982 and 2007(August).

Tony inherited his brother Chris's old Pentax and took a few shots while on a trip to Malaysia in 1982. Photography became a passion and changed his life.

This is his second Photographic Book.

Tony is a professional photographer working for corporate and private clients. He also paints

He is married to Isabelle and has one son, Maxim

tony@arnold-photo.co.uk / www.arnold-photo.co.uk

Prints are available from www.richmondphotos.co.uk

THE BRIDGE
AND
RIVERSIDE

13

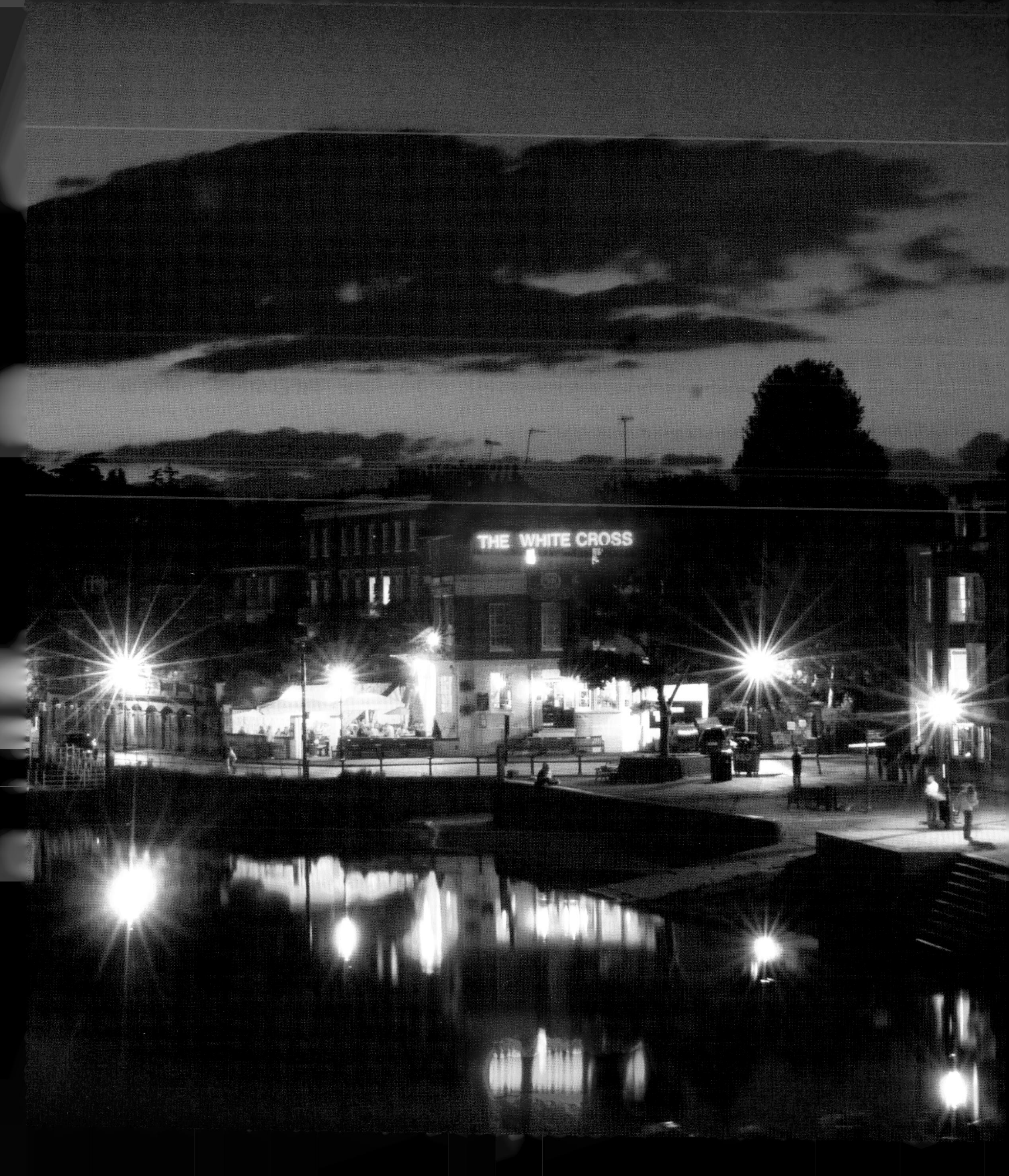
THE WHITE CROSS

RICHMOND HILL

ARCHITECTURAL
RICHMOND

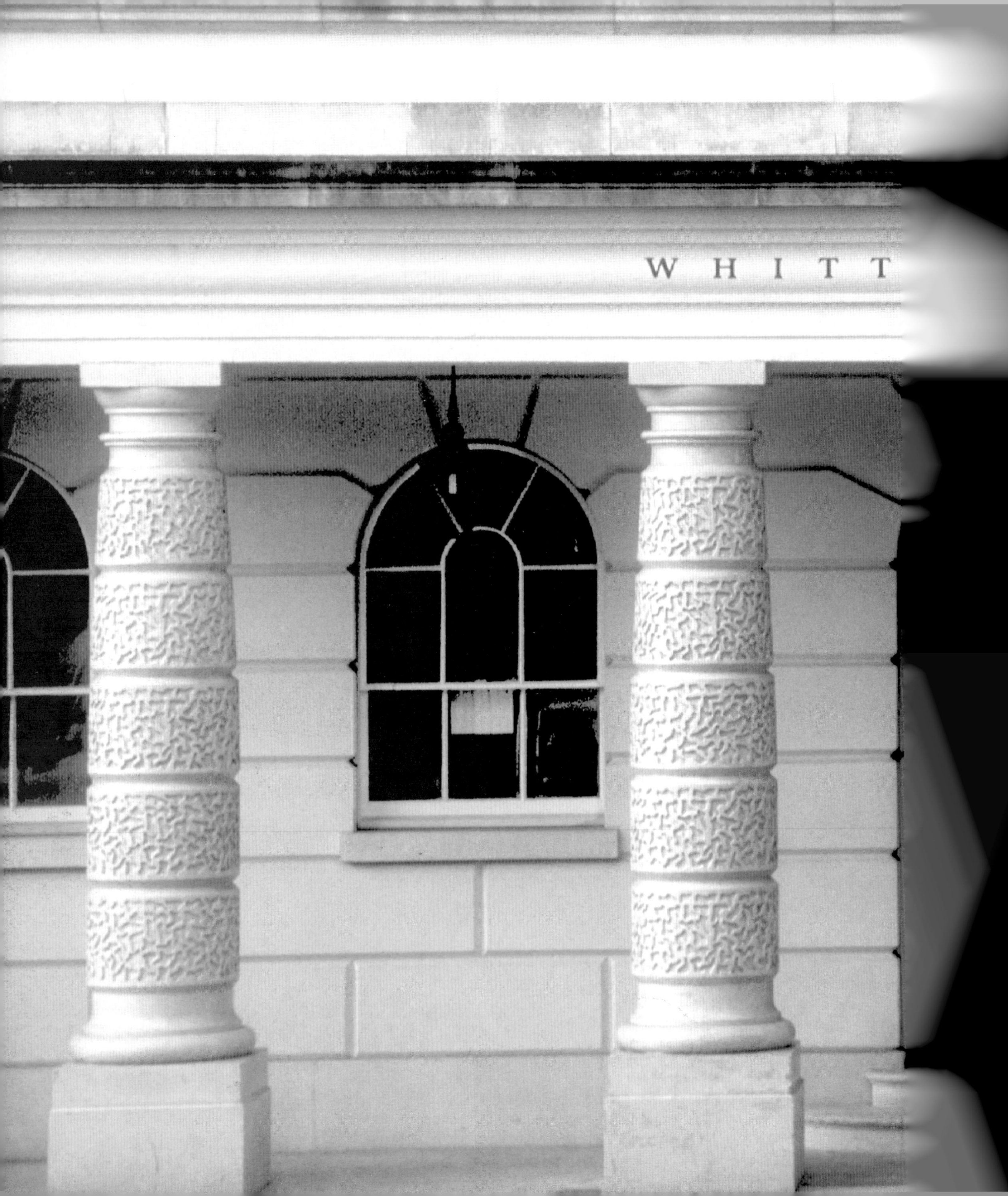
W H I T T

ART THEATRE MUSIC

40.50
HILL STREET

THE TOWN CENTRE

COIN DE PARIS

...SSERIE   CAFÉ   SANDW...

Major, Son & Phipps

MAJOR
Son & Phipps
ESTATE AGENT...
020 8940 2233

ALL
BAR
ONE

an exceedingly good place

stone bak...
pizza
by the yard

J•Y

Noble Jone...

100

ano's

Upstairs is the Italian Dining Room

buon appetito

vintage Italian wines

Brunello Di Montalcino - Barolo - Amarone - Tignanello

Chez Li

· RESTAURANT BRETON · CR

dsay

PERIE · RESTAURANT BRETON

NEXT
ALL DAY
BREAKFAST
only
3.95
ALSO T. AWAY
first on the
left
coffee

112

THE PARK

149

For the technically minded the photographs in this book
were taken on Nikon 35mm equipment and in part on medium
format Mamiya and Bronica cameras.
For black and white images: film stock Ilford HP5 and FP4
Images over the last 4 years taken on digital Nikons

Two images were taken on a Yashicamat.
One image was taken on a 5x4 Sinar Camera of Quinlan Terry's Development.

Tony Arnold August 2007